AF267228

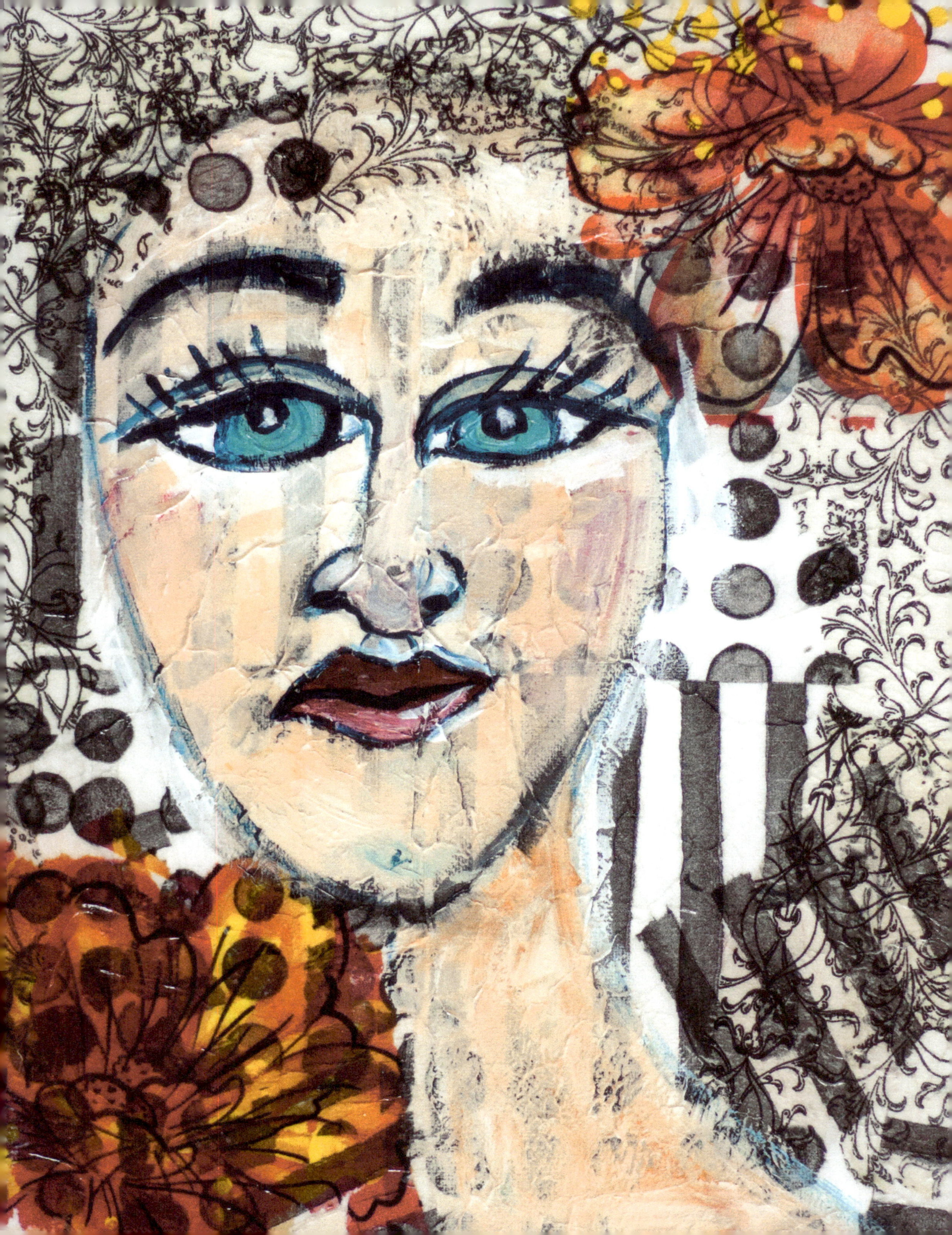

Dedicated to Tribe PMH for love and support on this incredible journey.

*And to my inspiring daughter
Emily Makenzie Hall*

*And to my darling mother
Cora Lee Phillips*

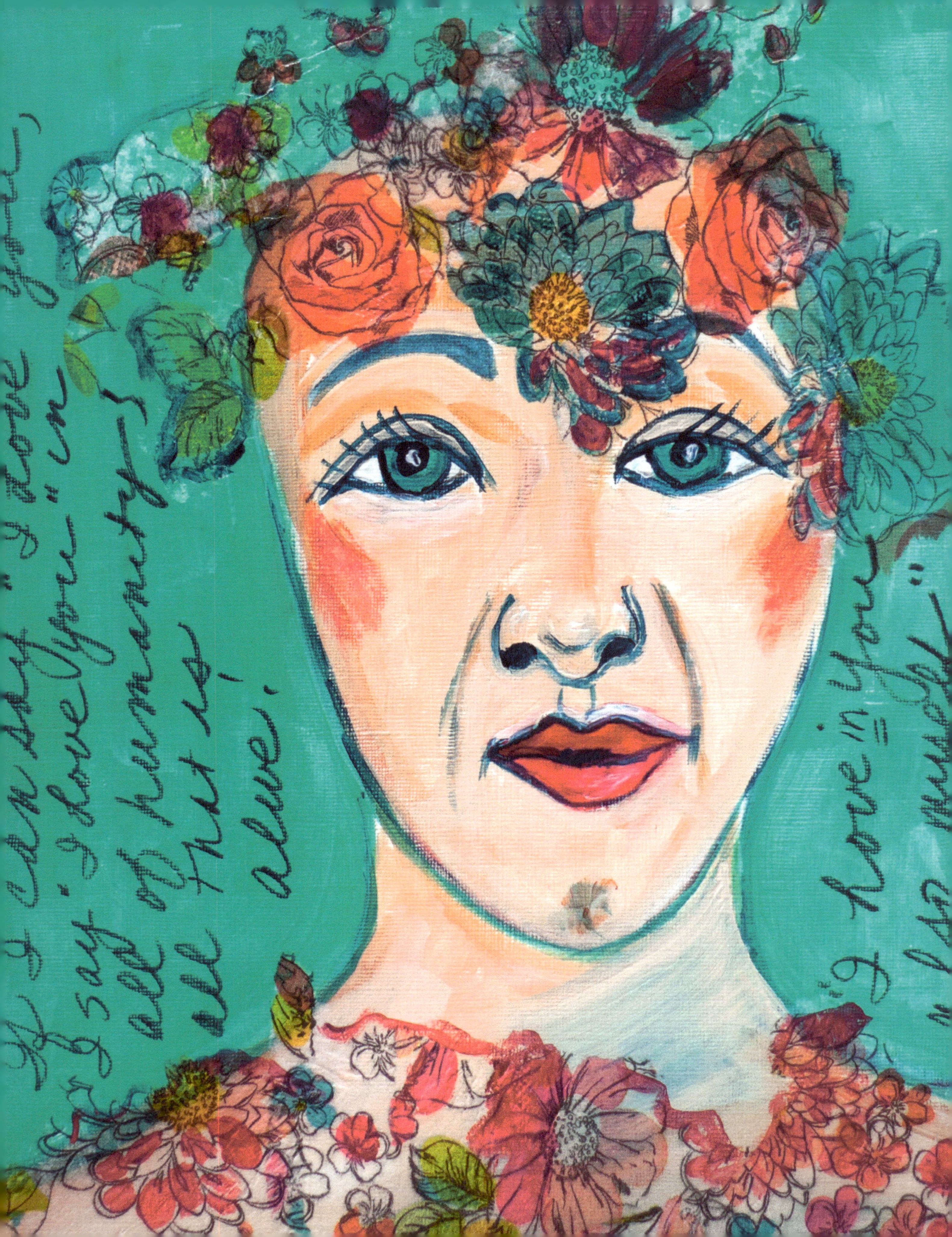

FORWARD

As Boomers entering our golden years, it is common to wonder if our lives still matter. What is it that we still have to offer? We face the challenges of careers ending, finances fluctuating, abilities diminishing and increasing responsibilities of caring for our aged parents as well as our own health and longevity. The lyrics and paintings in this book came to life through experiences and conversations about making decisions, choices and taking action. The fear of failing paralyzes a person from taking action at all. We want lives full of purpose and success. How do we achieve that?

The lyrics and stories in this book are companion to a group of songs I recorded as the album "Mangle the Tango." These songs talk about taking the risk to dream and do. Taking baby steps towards our visions, and risking that we will "Mangle the Tango," because "it's better to fall than never dance at all." It's not about perfection, it is about being faithful to step out, no matter what our age, and exercise whatever gifts we are able to tap into.

Some of the paintings in the book are directly tied to a song, others were just painted in the glow of inspiration of writing and recording the songs.

My main desire with these songs and paintings is to encourage you that you do matter, and to light a fire under your vision for your life. We are never too old to dream. So let's take a risk together to step into our next adventure even if we "Mangle the Tango."

The book is a companion to the "Mangle the Tango" CD which can be purchased at **manglethetango**.com   The book may be viewed alone or while playing the "Mangle the Tango" CD.

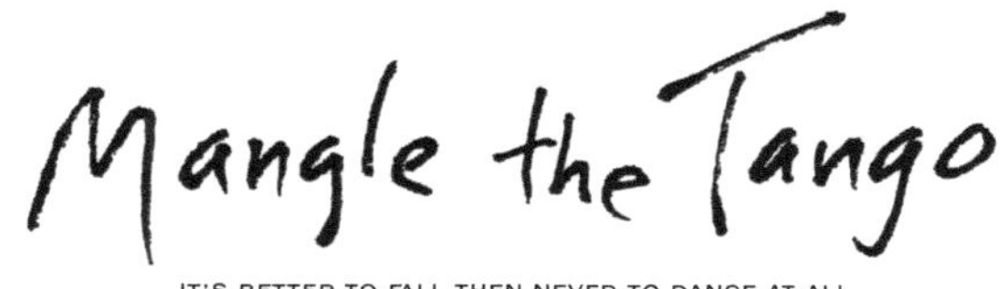

You can reach Pam for bookings at:
pmh@pammarkhall.com

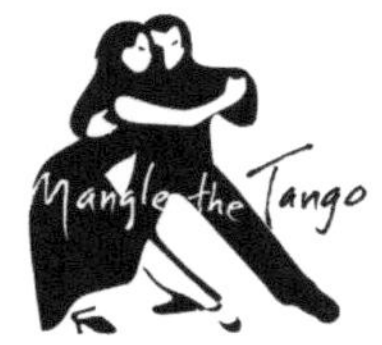

manglethetango.com

ISBN: 978-0-9977758-6-0

All Illustrations
Pam Mark Hall

Book Design
timmyroland.com

Mangle the Tango

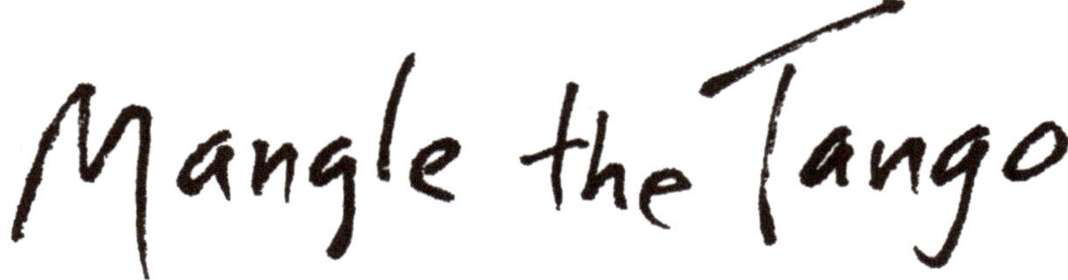

IT'S BETTER TO FALL THEN NEVER TO DANCE AT ALL

PAM MARK HALL

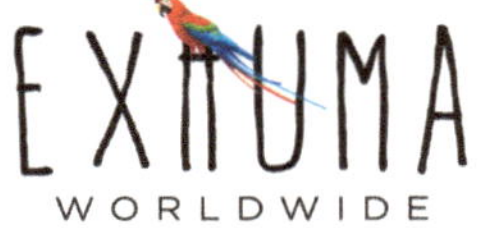

EXHUMA

WORLDWIDE

You can really light the world

When you love them

give yourself away

You're like a shining star

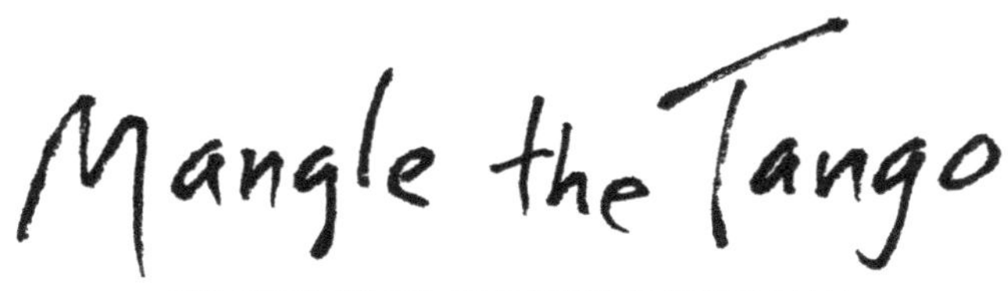

IT'S BETTER TO FALL THEN NEVER TO DANCE AT ALL

PLAYLIST

———

MANGLE THE TANGO

FALL FORWARD

HOW DO YOU KNOW?/COBALT BLUE

PERFECTLY IMPERFECT

CHOP WOOD, CARRY WATER

HELP ME PAPA

JOY RUNS DEEP
with Noel Paul Stookey

HARRIET TUBMAN
with the Sojourners

VERY LAST DAY
with Peter Yarrow

SOLITUDE

ALL THE DIAMONDS
with Bruce Cockburn

MANGLE THE TANGO
Pam Mark Hall

Perfectionism lies. Perfectionism kills creativity. Perfectionism ruins relationships. Perfectionism steals the magic of a perfectly imperfect moment.

How many times have you thought of something you'd love to learn or do only to be thwarted by that internal voice that warns you are too old, too out of date, you've had your turn, you aren't that smart, you aren't pretty enough, you're too fat or out of shape, people will laugh at you, your family thinks you are weird and a loser.

I wrote this song for a friend who continually sabotaged himself from achieving what he was gifted to do, by not starting unless he knew every little detail met his level of expectation. Consequently, he seldom began anything due to inertia. This song was me saying "Let's get up and dance even if in doing so we might 'Mangle the Tango.'

Recently, I had a realization that I myself had let perfectionism handicap me for years. I'd listened to all the voices I named above, and felt I'd lost all purpose and direction. I came to realize the message of "Mangle the Tango" was for me. Stop listening to those brutal internal voices, be kind and gentle to yourself. Take baby steps. Success is taking the first step and then another. I don't have to be da Vinci, but I will pick up a paintbrush and begin. I don't have to be Joni Mitchell, but I have the talent and ability to write lyrics and melodies. Success is picking up my guitar, or sitting down at the piano. I don't have to be the best, I just have to begin and continue til I'm done.

I will decide what to do and then begin one baby step at a time, even if it happens that I "Mangle the Tango. It's better to fall than never to dance at all."

It's your turn to lead
My turn to follow
So push or pull me like there's no tomorrow
Let's not waste the dance debating the right way to begin
Even if we mangle the tango

Feel the music, oh, so mesmerizing
Gaze into my eyes while improvising
Defy the fear of falling or tumbling as we spin
Even if we mangle the tango

Chorus
Even if we mangle the tango
Oh, there's one thing I know
It's better to fall
Than never to dance at all
Let's dance!

Hold me close then let me move beside you
Let's lift our heads, oh steady now, we can do,
If we take four steps and then pause
We'll make it 'cross the room
Even if we mangle the tango

Mangle the Tango

Mangle the Tango
There's one thing I know
Its better
to fall
Than
Never to
Dance at all
Take a
risk to
mangle
The
Tango

Inspired by a
a commencement speech by **Denzel Washington**

FALL FORWARD
Pam Mark Hall

One night I was checking out posts on Facebook and also browsing the news. Somehow I came upon the commencement speech Denzel Washington gave to a graduating class from University of Pennsylvania.

I was so taken by what he was saying that I watched it a second time and wrote out everything he said. The very next morning I went straight to my piano and began and playing and singing "Fall Forward."

The basic message is that everyone who attempts to do anything will fail at one point or another. If you don't fail sometime it means you are not even trying at all.

Keep taking risks, keep putting yourself out there. And when you fall, don't fall backwards into despair and beat yourself up. Fall forward, keep trying, keep reaching, keep hoping.

When I fail, or get discouraged, I am tempted to fall backward into a hole and become despondent. This message encourages me to see it all as a part of the process of becoming who I want to be. It goes hand in hand with the message of "Chop Wood, Carry Water." Pick yourself back up and do the next right thing. That might be washing dishes, making the bed, practicing a song, calling a friend, et. al . Just keep moving forward.

Mangle the Tango

Don't hold back now give it all you got
Take a risk in time that you might fall a lot
You're not too young or old to give your best
Never too late to rise above the test
Let nothing stop you from learning, growing
Let nothing stop you from loving, hoping
Listen up to what I say
Gotta push that fear away
Lean into it all, when you fall just

Fall Forward
Fall Ever Free
Fall Forward
Toward the Mercy
Fall Forward

You're gonna lose sometimes, embarrass yourself
You're gonna fail, it's true, like everybody else
The best advice is to embrace the fall
If you don't fail you didn't try at all
Here's what to do when your ship has sailed, darlin'
Here's what to do when your through with wailin'
Pick your self back up and pray
Don't fall back, don't go down that way
Lean into it all, and when you fall just

Fall Forward
Fall Ever Free
Fall Forward
Toward the Mercy
Fall Forward

Take a risk 'bout what you know
Take a risk 'bout where you go
Take a risk with who you meet
Take a risk with the way you see
Hold lightly to the things you own
Step out your comfort zone
Try to think with an open mind
You'll be surprised at what you find

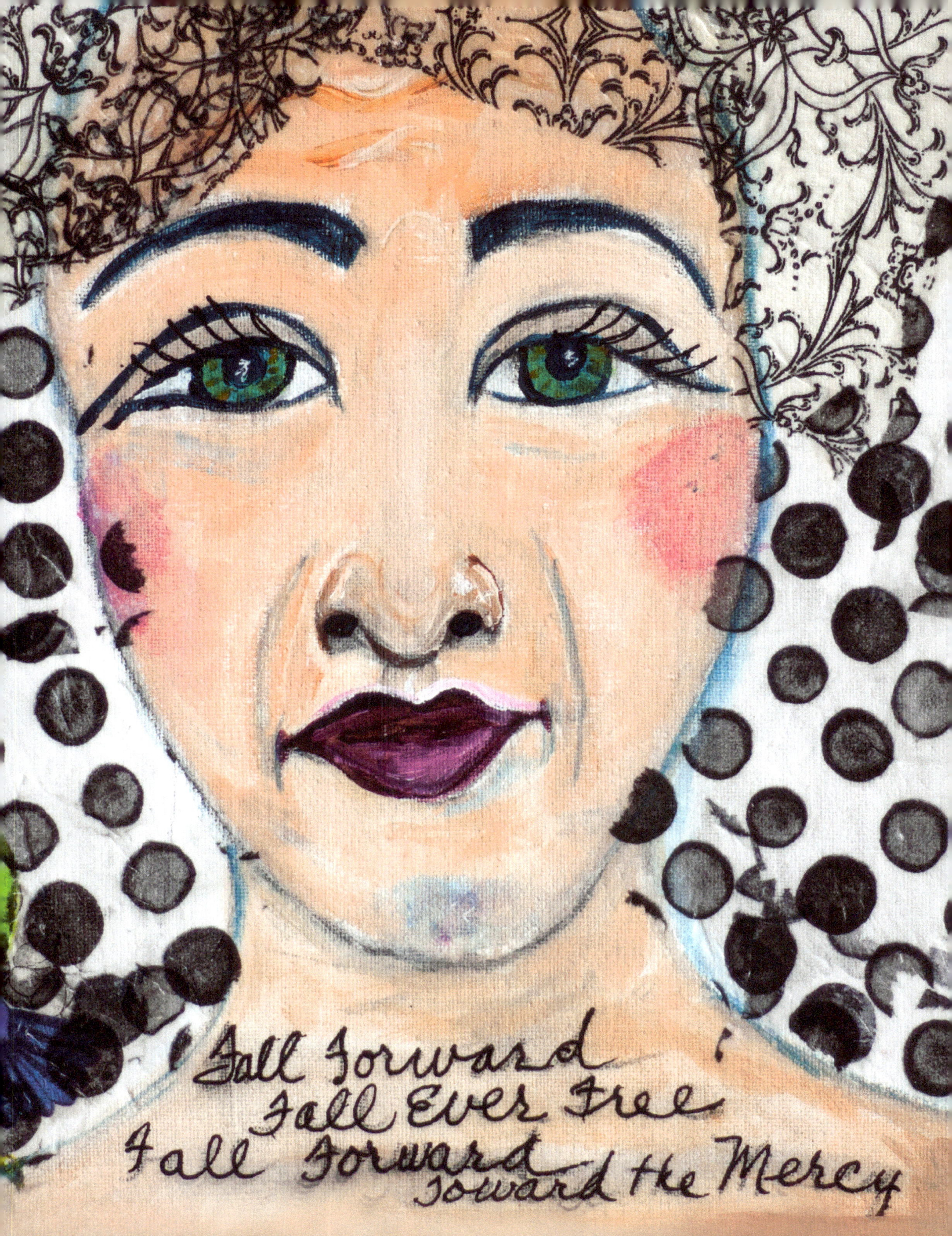
Fall Forward
Fall Ever Free
Fall Forward
Toward the Mercy

HOW DO YOU KNOW [COBALT BLUE]
Pam Mark Hall

This is a timely song written specifically to challenge the mudslingers in the recent presidential campaigns. Unfortunately, I've lost a few friends due to unsubstantiated accusations and an unwillingness to abide my different point of view.

This conflict brought to mind my friend, Jackie, who years before went to study at Frances Schaeffer's L'Abri with the burning question "How do you know that you know?" My version of the question became "How do you know that you what you know?" I agree that we'd be pretty out of sync if we couldn't be confident that we know something based on facts. But it is a good to check ourselves when we are throwing our opinions around to challenge ourselves about the basis of our views.

The sub-title is "Cobalt Blue." Cobalt blue represents mystery. It's ok for us to embrace that it is not a cop-out to embrace mystery within our search for truth.

Mangle the Tango

Whistling past the graveyard ghosts
So I don't hear them speak
Fumbling with futility
Am I doomed to repeat
All the wreckage left in the
Ancestral wake?

Creeping fast like Kudzu
Thoughts are swallowing my life
Strangling existence
Till I pull out the knife
Slash back the voices
Take back my space and mind

Chorus
How do you know
That you know
What you know?
How do you know
That you know What You Know?

Cobalt Blue, Juggle and Swoon
Cobalt Blue

Take a flying leap to find relief
In the here and now
In the beauty of the gloaming
The paradox of how
At one time
I can both fall and fly

Chorus

Truth de noir, so darkly seen
Truth de noir, the Mystery

Comment savez-vous que
Vous savez ce que Vous savez?

Chorus

Cobalt Blue, Juggle and Swoon
Cobalt Blue, Juggle and Swoon

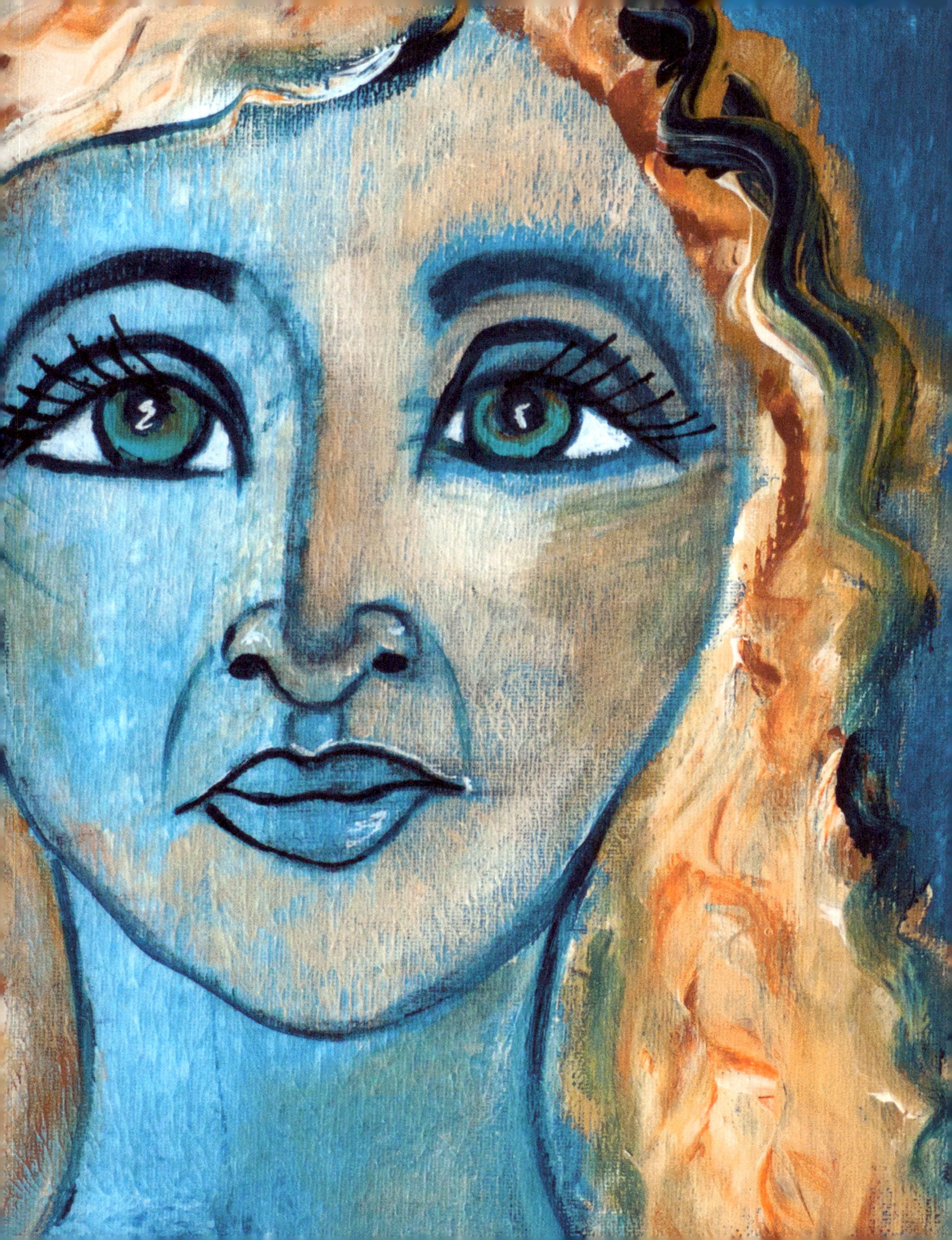

PERFECTLY IMPERFECT
Pam Mark Hall

Oh gosh. Acceptance, gratitude, beauty, and joy are all words that come to mind about this song. Sometimes circumstances seem overwhelming and all-consuming. It is easy to sink into feelings of despair when life isn't the way I imagined it would be or should be. It's easy to look at all the things or opportunities I don't have and feel despondent.

I'm a hot mess. But I'm also special. There are so many things I don't know how to do, like navigate technology very well, but there are some things that I do quite well. I am learning how to give myself permission to congratulate myself on a job well done. I am learning to be gentle with myself when I go round in circles trying to fix something I don't know much about.

I lived out of suitcases and friends' guest rooms for three years after the great recession hit and I lost my job and ability to pay my mortgage. Just stating it sounds so pitiful, but the reality is that those three years provided me the opportunity to become close to friends I'd known all my life from a distance. This provided me the opportunity to experience family and real "church." It is a season of life that I am so grateful for as God's provisions became so clear to me.

I am now grateful for a 1980 doublewide smack dab in a mobile home community for folks over 55. Never in a million years could I have imagined that I would find such peace and beauty in such a venue. But my back porch faces an open field and I have birds on the feeders all day long singing to me and each other. I am inspired every day to rise with a smile. I'm inspired to write new songs. I'm inspired to paint. I'm inspired to care for my aging parents. And I'm inspired to care for others.

This is not how I thought my life would go. I figured that I'd build success upon success and have a real house and stability. I have learned to be grateful and experience a richness in life not based on things. I've learned to find peace in my "Perfectly Imperfect" world.

Living in the lap of luxury
Right here in my double-wide
Got my books, my paints and piano
And a view of the field and sky
The birds they keep me company
A friendly fox occasionally
They make the best of neighbors
And they never ask for favors

It don't take lots of money
To live like royalty
Anyone can take pleasure
In a place where you find true leisure
Sometimes it's hard to make ends meet
The car breaks down, the plumbing leaks
And all that's left are beans to eat
But all in all right here and now

chorus
It's a Perfectly Imperfect Day
In a Perfectly Imperfect way
I may be down but I'm not out
I'm Perfectly Imperfect, hey
In a Perfectly Imperfect way

It ain't no Mar-a-Lago
But it's sure home to me
There's a pool up by the clubhouse
And I've got a key
Out my sliding glass back door
I couldn't ask for any more
I got acres of rolling green space
I got the time, I got the place

It's a Perfectly Imperfect day
in a Perfectly Imperfect way
I may be down but I'm not out
I'm Perfectly Imperfect, hey
In a Perfectly Imperfect way

There's beauty all around us
Enough for everyone
Start with a little gratitude
And sadness comes undone

Mangle the Tango

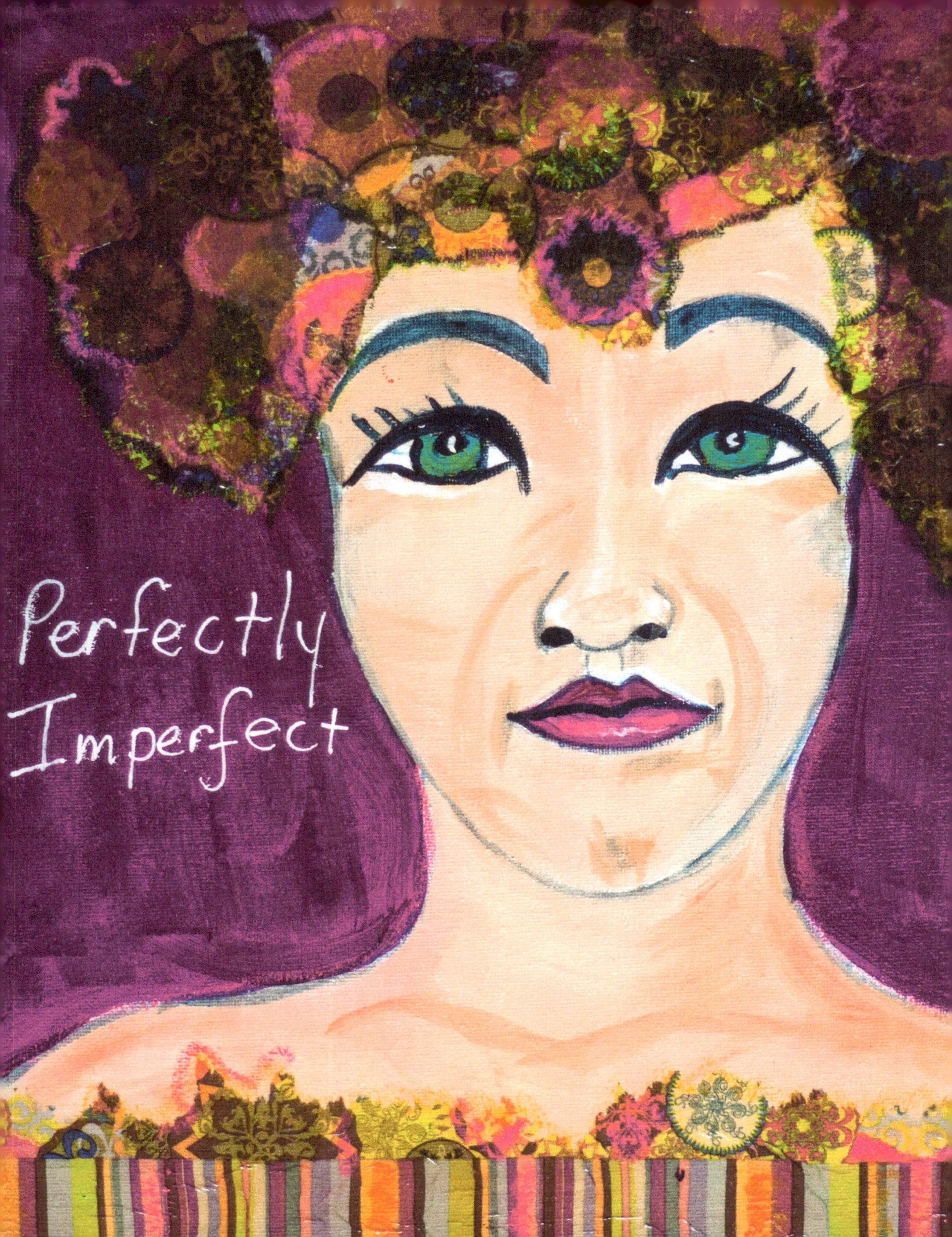

Perfectly
Imperfect

CHOP WOOD, CARRY WATER
Pam Mark Hall

One of my most current songs. I just finished writing it in January, 2017. I'd been mulling the saying over in my mind for months and then I found a book by the same title by a fellow named Joshua Medcalf. As soon as I began reading it, it resonated. I've marinated in the book, reading it over and over. While journaling, low and behold, lyrics formed.

It's the concept of being present and grateful in every moment and giving your best to the little things in your world that build your character and ultimately grows your greatness. Ultimately you'll "shine in the light what you refine in the dark."

For me that refining has taken years and years. I guess the idea that you have to "make it" by a certain age or there's no hope really fights against this concept. Now as a senior citizen, I'm ready to make certain things happen that I wasn't ready for when I was younger. As long as I've got tread on my tires I want to keep moving forward and creating. So back to practice, practice and more practice and being prepared for the moments I'm given to share my gifts.

Mangle the Tango

Chop Wood, Carry Water
One foot in front of the other
Every step or swing
Can make you stronger
Chop Wood, Carry Water
No task too small not to bother
Don't take the short cut
It can make the way harder

You had a dream
A real good dream
But you lost heart and
You lost hope
Well, you fell behind
Or so it seems
The only way forward is
Round and round and round

Chop Wood, Carry Water
One foot in front of the other
Every step or swing
Can make you stronger
Chop Wood, Carry Water
No task too small not to bother
Don't take the short cut
It can make the way harder

Go build your house
Go plant your field
Be faithful
In your daily dealings
Care for strangers
Care for friends
Even when it seems you go
Round and Round and Round

Now here you are
wiser, and kinder from
The work of your hands
The work of your heart
You'll shine in the light
What you refine in the dark

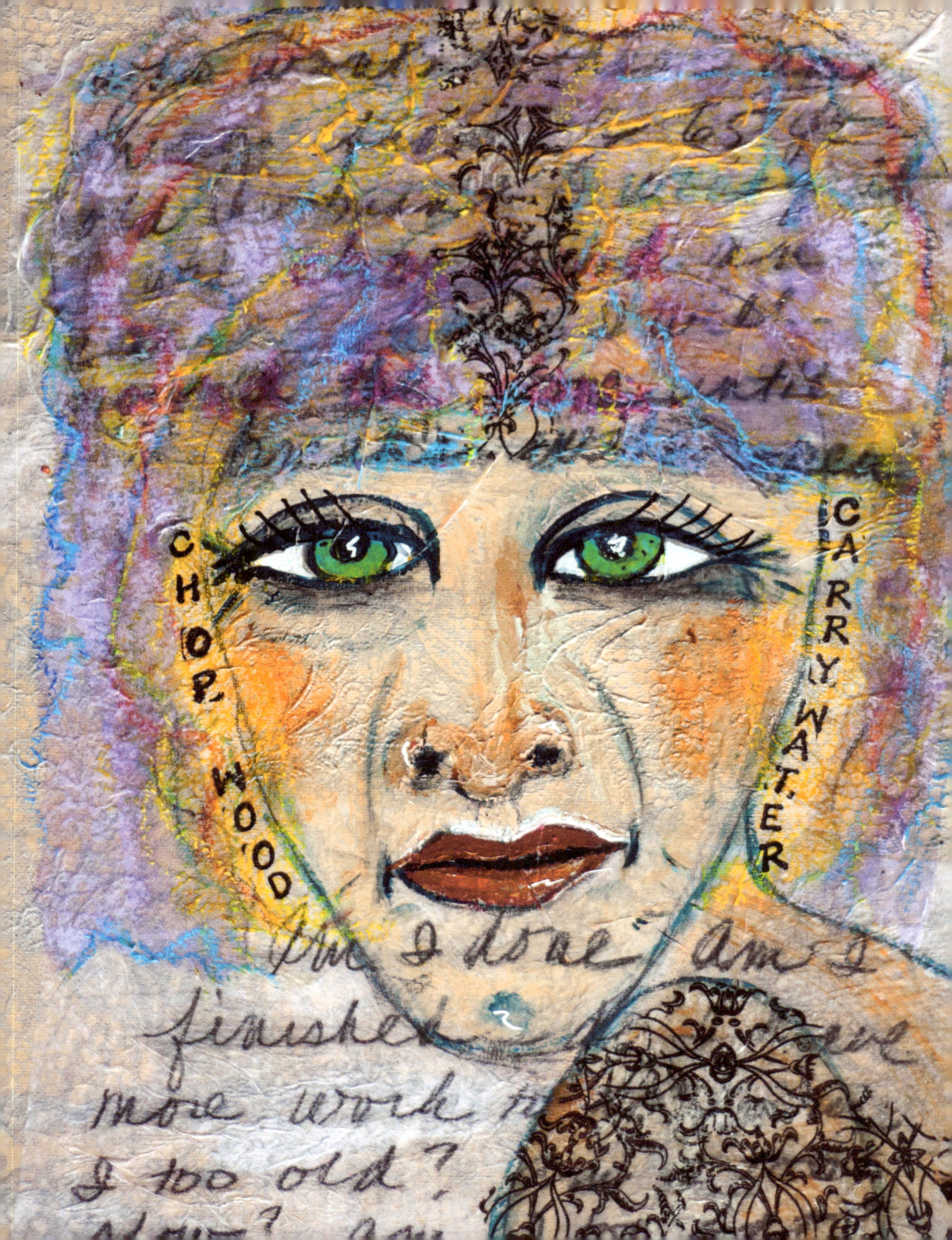

CHOP WOOD
CARRY WATER
Am I done? Am I
finished...
more work...
I too old?

*Inspired by the book **"The Shack"***

HELP ME PAPA

Pam Mark Hall

This song was inspired by the gut-wrenching questions of Mack, the protagonist of the book "The Shack". He wonders why, if God is so good, did God allow an evil man to kidnap and murder his precious little girl, Missy. This song is what I imagine Mack's conversation to be with God. It mirrors my own disillusionment and demanding of God to make sense of circumstances that seem to be at odds with the concept of God as good and loving. It wrestles with the age old question of if God is "in control" then why does God allow such evil in the world?

It is an uncomfortable dark song, for sure. It does not finish with a tidy answer, but it concludes with the acknowledgement that his "grief has left me weak and blind." A concession to faith that God's goodness is just not seen in that moment but there's still hope within the doubt.

My own "grief has left me weak and blind." I know that I don't see things clearly. There are so many dimensions to life. I see dimly. And because I know I see things dimly, I continue to embrace the belief that God is good and is with me as I grope my way through the dark.

When will my heart every mend
I cry the blues that never end
Like a meteor quickly I descend
And grieve the stars left in the sky
Is she with angels can she fly
Was she frightened when she died

Help Me Papa
To understand this tragedy
These thorns in my roses on the vine
I still wonder
Why You allowed such evil
Steal away this child of mine

I still hold her inside of me
Baptized in tears of my agony
I should let her rest in peace
I should let her go, give her release
But I keep waiting, hope to hear
Her laughter and her song so sweet and clear

Help Me Papa
To understand this tragedy
These thorns in my roses on the vine
I still wonder
Why You allowed such evil
Steal away this child of mine

Please explain every thread of this tapestry
As they twist, turn and weave their dark design
Shine Your light through the colors I can't see
My grief has left me weak and blind

Mangle the Tango

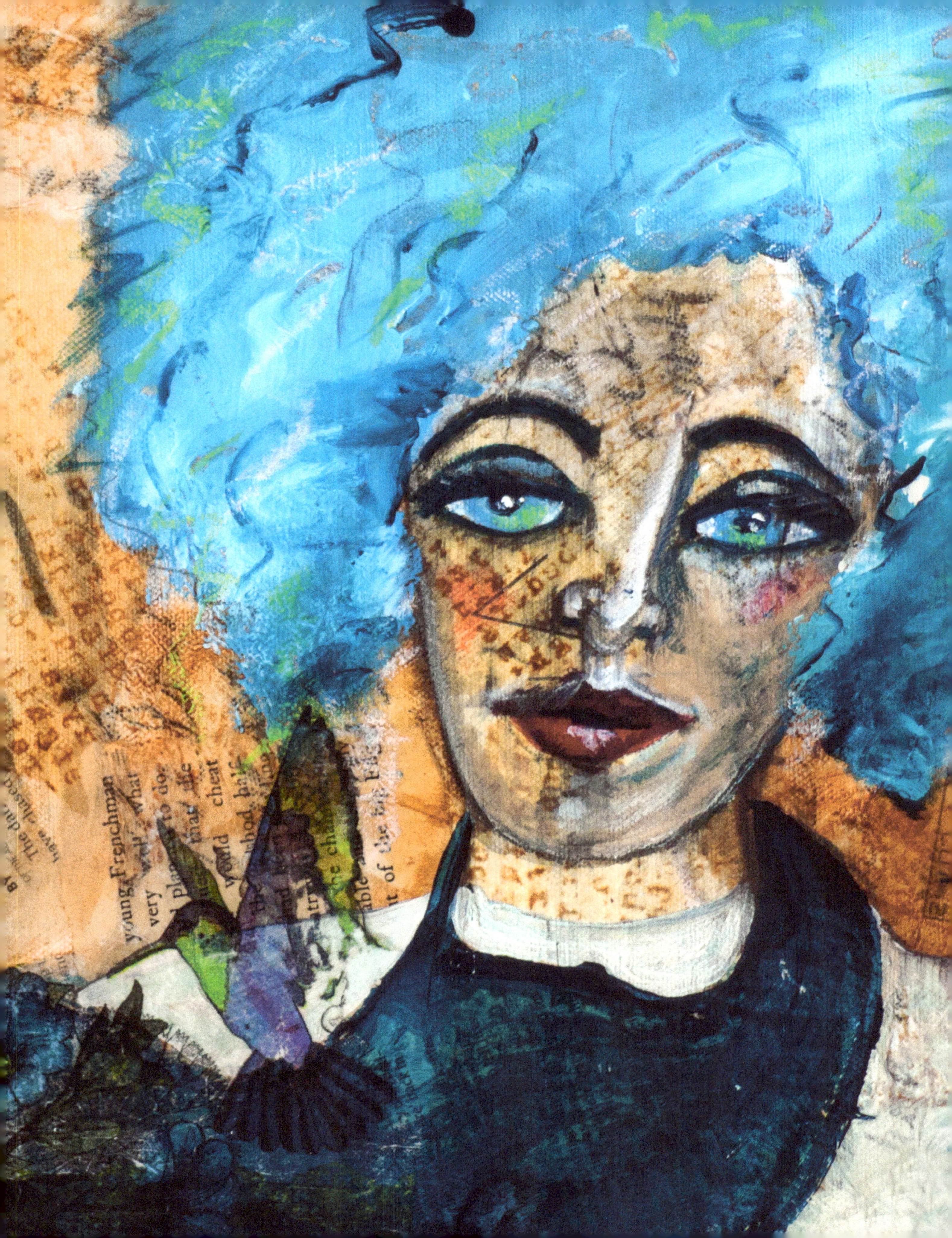
young Frenchman
very
to die.
cheat

JOY RUNS DEEP

Pam Mark Hall

C.S. Lewis wrote a partial autobiography called "Surprised by Joy: The Shape of My Early Life" published in 1955. Joy is not something that can be obtained by searching for it. I read it about 40 years ago and have carried the concept with me throughout my life. It is a by product of ones relationship with God and a sense of peace and purpose. It ebbs and flows and it surprises us sometimes when we least expect it.

I initially began writing "Joy Runs Deep" for a little girl who loves dolphins and Narnia. It evolved into a song that is for children and adults. I performed it at a fund raising concert in Nashville with students from the W.O. Smith School. The W.O. Smith School provides music lessons for 50 cents a lesson to children who otherwise couldn't afford it. The professional musicians in Nashville donate their time to give lessons.

I'm currently involved with a non-profit called Cyrus Music Foundation. They raise money for scholarships for children to take private music lessons. Since public schools have largely cut budgets for music programs, this is a crucial service provided to the community.

Mangle the Tango

Sometimes at night you travel when you sleep
Swimming with dolphins
Diving low and then you leap out the blue
To seek adventure
Twisting and twirling to see and to be seen
Delighted you giggle gliding through a tide of green
Gravity pulls and you surrender

Joy runs deep, joy runs deep
Out of sight, out of mind
Always a surprise at how it finds you
Joy runs deep, Joy runs deep
Why don't you let it come, let it go
Surging through the ebb and flow of life

You wake in the morning brave and curious
Facing the world even though it may be dangerous
Still life is good, always remember
Learning and growing to be all you can be
Sometimes you struggle reaching for your hopes and dreams
Destiny calls and it surrenders

Joy runs deep, joy runs deep
Out of sight, out of mind
Always a surprise at how it finds you
Joy runs deep, Joy runs deep
Why don't you let it come, let it go
Surging through the ebb and flow of life

Life is sacred you understand
It's a gift, embrace it while you can
There's so much to receive with open hands

Joy runs deep, joy runs deep
Out of sight, out of mind
Always a surprise at how it finds you
Joy runs deep, Joy runs deep
Why don't you let it come, let it go
Surging through the ebb and flow
Let it come, let it go
Find you in the undertow
Let it come, let it go
Surging through the ebb and flow of life

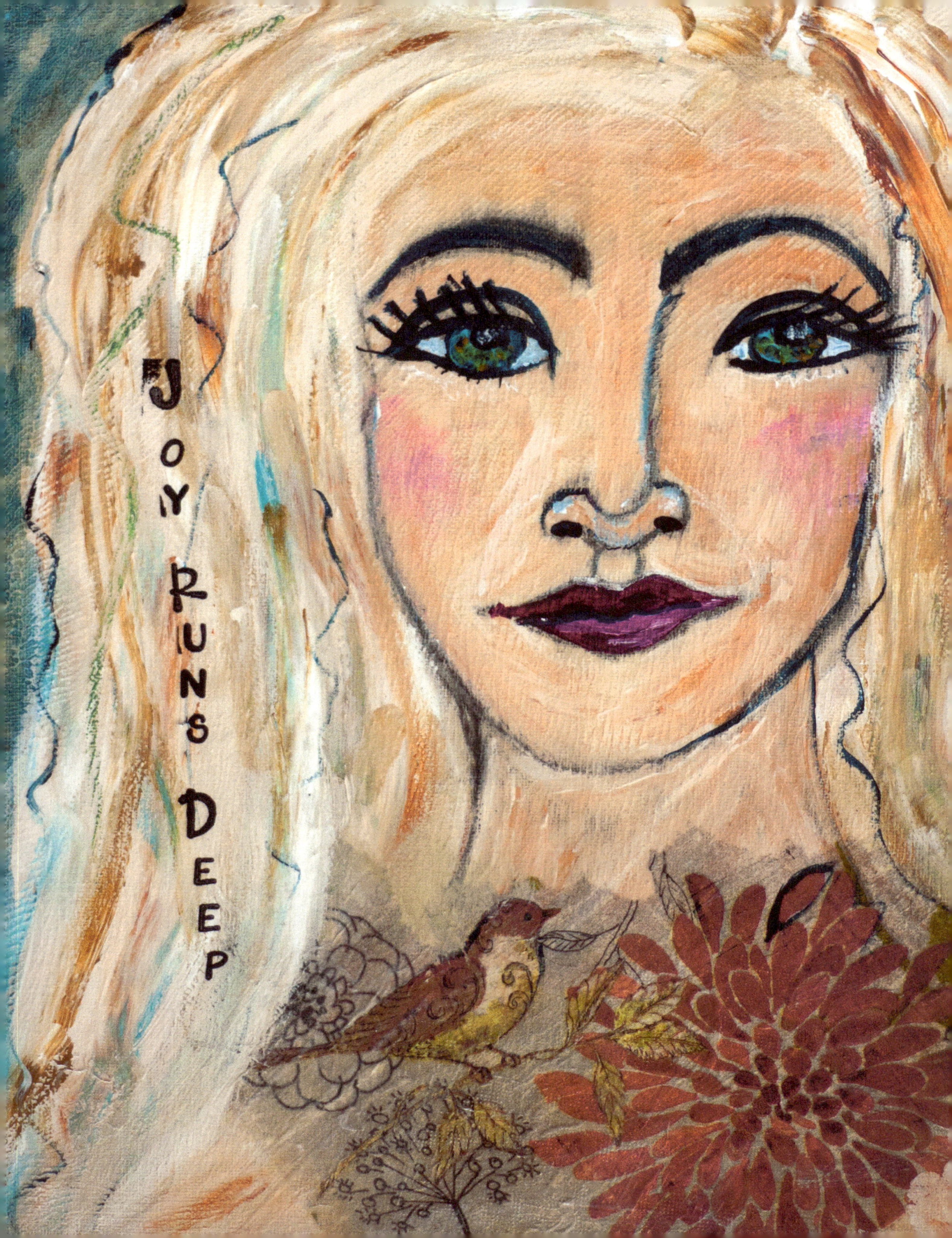

JOY RUNS DEEP

HARRIET TUBMAN
Walter Robinson

This is a song I first heard Kate Taylor sing back in the late 70's. Right then and there I adopted it as my own. The story of Harriet Tubman has been a constant reminder of how personal freedom is not only for personal comfort and security. Harriet Tubman won her own freedom and then did the unthinkable. She went back into enemy territory to rescue other slaves and lead them out into freedom as well. She lived for a purpose larger than herself. She is a constant reminder to reach outside myself and in the little ways I can to lighten the load of others.

I'll be singing this song when I'm 90 if God grants me that long and a voice to sing it.

One night I dreamed I was in slavery
'Bout 1850 was the time
Sorrow was the only sign
Nothin' around to ease my mind
Out of the night appeared a lady
Leading a distant pilgrim band
First mate she yelled pointing her hand
Make room aboard for this young woman

Chorus

She said:
Come on up I got a lifeline
Come on up to this train of mine
Come on up I got a lifeline
Come on up to this train of mine
She said her name was Harriet Tubman
And she drove for the underground railroad

Hundreds of miles we travelled onward
Gatherings slaves from town to town
Seeking every lost and found
Setting those free that once were bound

Somehow my heart was growing weaker
I fell by the wayside sinking sand
Firmly did this lady stand
She lifted me up and took my hand

Chorus

Who are those children dressed in red
Must be the ones that Moses led
Who are those children dressed in red
Must be the ones that Moses led

Chorus

Mangle the Tango

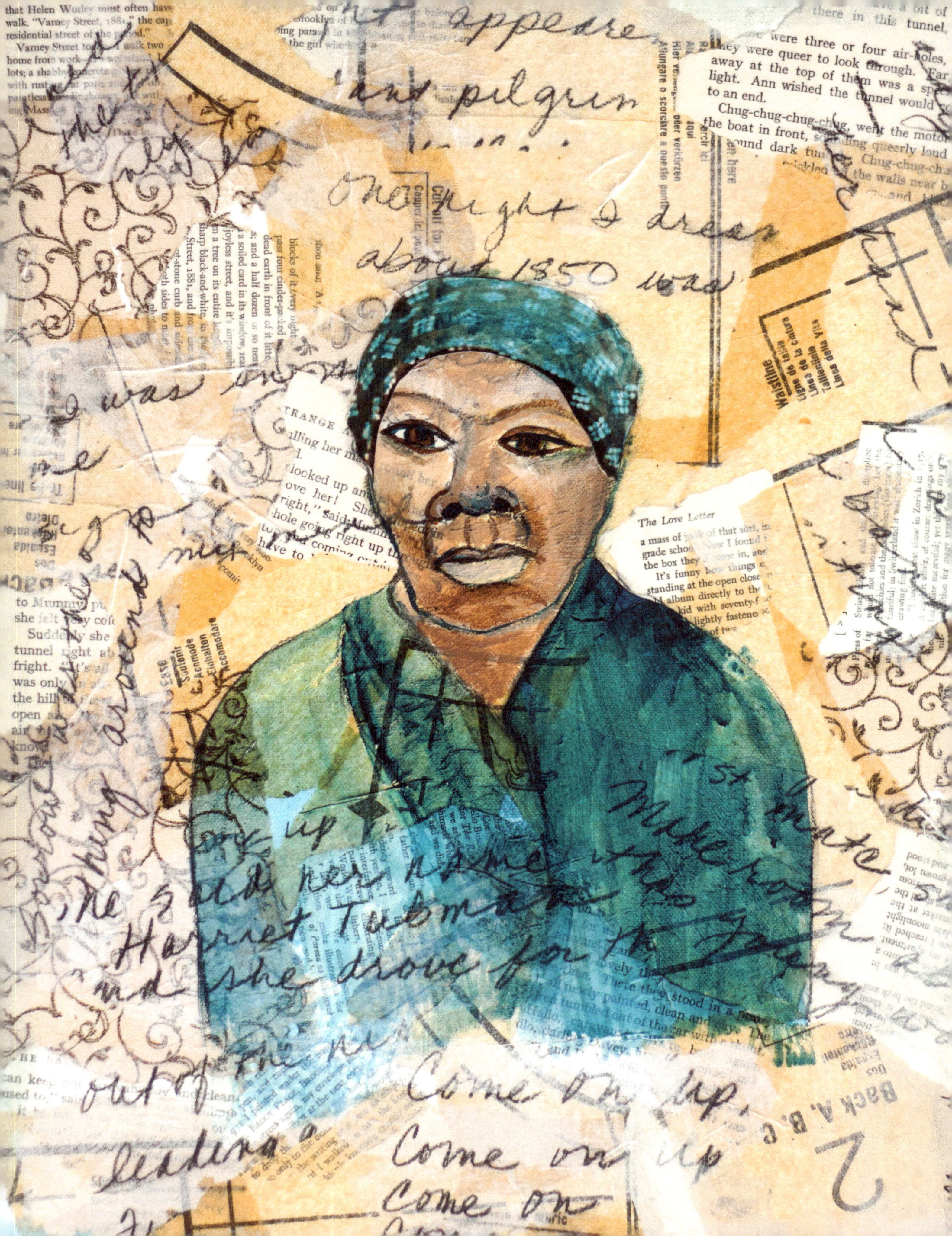

one night I dream
about 1850 was
She said her name was
Harriet Tubman
and she drove for the
out of the
Come on up,
Come on up
Come on

VERY LAST DAY

Paul Stookey & Peter Yarrow

When I was twelve years old I begged my mother to buy me a guitar. She finally consented. She purchased it out of the Sacramento Bee and had it shipped from San Francisco sight unseen. It was a beautiful guitar, but it had strings about an inch up off the neck. There was no way I could push the strings down with one hand, so I enlisted the help of my best friend, Vicki Stringfellow. I would position the fingers of my left hand on the proper frets and strings and then push it down with my right hand while Vicki strummed. It hurt like heck. But I can tell you I built up some pretty great callouses.

I bought a Peter, Paul and Mary songbook and one of the first songs we learned was "The Very Last Day." We practiced and practiced. Convincing my mother I was serious about playing guitar, she took me down to Valley Music and she let me pick out a nylon string guitar. It was heavenly to play. It was an Aria.

Vicki and I formed a folk singing group called the "Townfolk Singers." We sang tons of Peter, Paul and Mary, Bob Dylan, Gordon Lightfoot, New Christy Minstrels and others. Of course I idolized Peter, Paul and Mary and would fantasize about singing with them.

Fast forward ten years and I had continued pursuing music as a career. I had the delight of doing a concert in Long Beach Auditorium with my mentor, John Fischer, and Noel Paul Stookey of Peter Paul and Mary. Over the years Noel and I have maintained our friendship, have written and recorded together. Over the past couple of years we performed at a private event and recently he recorded a duet with me on "Joy Runs Deep."

Top that off with Peter Yarrow joined me to record "The Very Last Day" - one of the first songs I ever learned to play. How special is that?

Mangle the Tango

Everybody gonna pray
On the very last day
When they hear the bell
Ring the world away
Everybody gonna pray
To the heavens on the judgement day

Oh, you can sing about your great king David
You can preach about the wisdom of Saul
But judgement falls on all mankind
When the trumpet sounds the call
All equal and the same
When the Lord he calls your name
Get ready brother for that day

Well one day soon all men will stand,
His word will be heeded in all the land
Men shall know and men shall see
We all are brothers and we all are free
Mankind was made of clay
Each of us in the very same way
Get ready, brother, for that day

Everybody gonna pray
On the very last day
When they hear the bell
Ring the world away
Everybody gonna pray
To the heavens on the judgement day

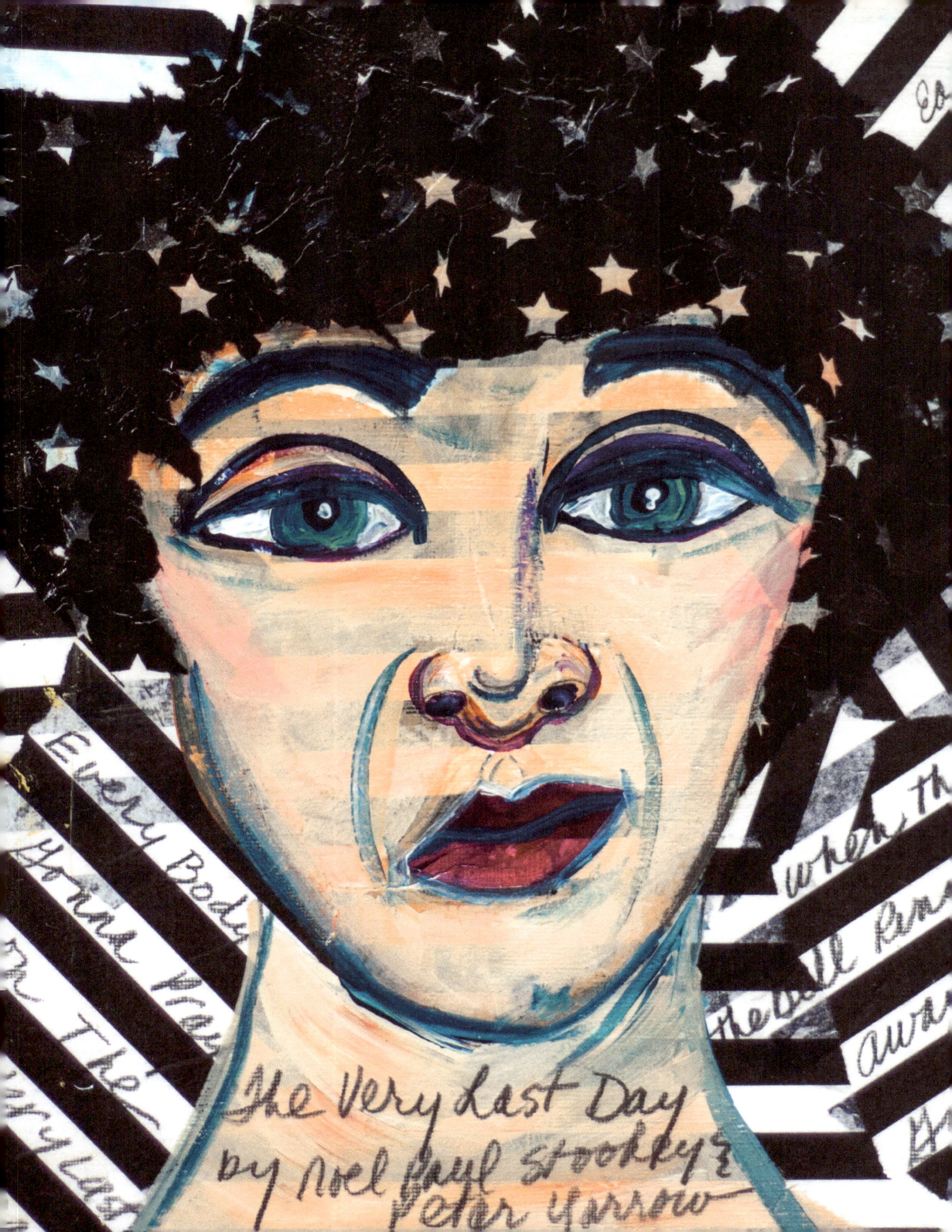
Every Body
The Very Last Day
by noel paul stookey &
peter yarrow
when th
the will Ris
awa

SOLITUDE

Pam Mark Hall

In 1995-1998 I worked for the TN State Coalition Against Domestic Violence. Prior to that I'd worked for the Nashville Salvation Army 1991-1995. In 1987, I'd gone through a divorce, lost my record deal and the invitations to come perform or "minister" stopped. Music ministry is the only work I'd done my entire adult life and because as a divorced woman, I no longer qualified as a worthy minister, I also lost my only means of livelihood. I went from singing in front of thousands to cleaning houses, hanging wallpaper, teaching myself decorative painting and marketing myself to dr.'s offices, recording studios, and labels. I actually faux-finished the office of Warner Bros. Christian Music. My world was turned on it's head.

After 7 years of hard work with no time off of any sort, I put my things in storage in Nashville, and rented a room on Martha's Vineyard for the summer. I walked on the beach, I met locals, went to art openings, spent a lot of time alone writing songs and in my journal.

I cherished my solitude and wrote a song about that state. One of my favorite lines is "Solitude, oh what a simple pleasure, a poor girl's luxury." My solitude was a beautiful luxury. It was a once in a lifetime luxury on that idyllic island. When I need to go to my "happy place" that's where I go to in my mind.

Solitude
My deepest darkest secret
Like a lover take me home
Seduce my heart with a silent whisper
Now that we are all alone
Inside out or turn me outside in
Anyway you wanna look at where I've been
I've been up down all around
Full circle I begin
Seeking jewels in solitude

Solitude
Oh what a simple pleasure
A poor girl's luxury
Shake my soul
Startle me to my senses
With fragrant memories
Earth and sky I saw them
Sand and sea
Light and color kissing shamelessly
Oh drench these dry bones
Craving beauty
Seeking Jewels in Solitude

Solitude
Mystical meditation, timeless remedy
Eye to eye that's how you always find me
Floating in your treasury
When they call be back to face
The day's reality
All the boats the China couldn't carry me
And all the beauty I found inside of me
Seeking jewels in solitude

Mangle the Tango

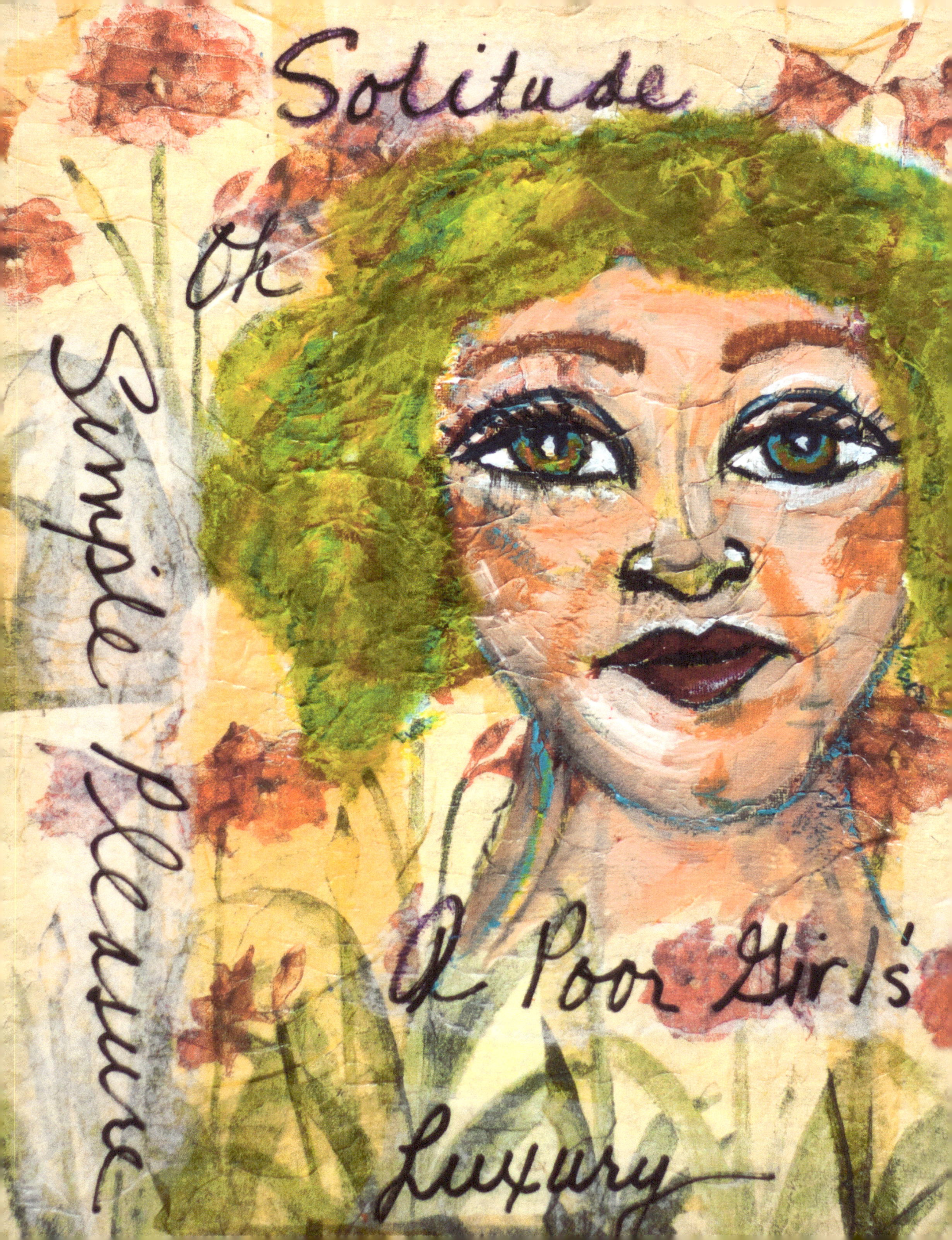

Solitude
Oh
Simple pleasure
A Poor Girl's
Luxury

ALL THE DIAMONDS
Bruce Cockburn

I lived in Nashville for 32 years. One of my favorite things to do was to walk a mile around a man-made reservoir called Radnor Lake. It was created to contain the water for the steam-train yard located about a mile away. It is a gorgeous state park that is treasured by the locals for the trails that wind through pines and deciduous trees and provide frequent glimpses of wildlife i.e. deer, turtles, geese, ducks.

I began walking there when my daughter was a toddler and it was one of our favorite outings. One of the things that a jaunt through the woods can do is to bring songs to mind from the depths of our memories.

Every time I walked at Radnor and saw the sunlight sparkling on the surface of the lake, Bruce Cockburn's song "All the Diamonds in the World" would begin singing itself and I'd join in. That song is ever embedded in my memory as belonging to my Radnor Lake/Emily Hall experience.

I've wanted to record it for many years. I recorded another Bruce Cockburn song back in the 70's on my Star Song Records release "Never Fades Away." Label head Darrell Harris introduced me to Bruce's "Lord of the Starfields" which I immediately deemed as an expression of my own heart and voice. It remains one of the favorite songs and performances of my career.

Bruce Cockburn and I later became friends when I interviewed him for a radio show I hosted on a top 40 radio station in Portland, OR. We've maintained that friendship over the many years and miles. I was thrilled he said "yes" when I contacted him to ask him if I could record "All the Diamonds in the World" and if he'd play guitar and sing on the track. We tracked his guitars and vocals at the famous Fantasy Studios in Berkeley, CA. I felt I was in a dream for he has been a person, songwriter, performer and activist that I've admired and been inspired by since my 20's. What a gift.

All the diamonds in this world
That mean anything to me
Are conjured up by wind and sunlight
Sparkling on the sea

I ran aground in a harbor town
Lost the taste for being free
Thank God He sent some gull-chased ship
To carry me to sea

Two thousand years and half a world away
Dying trees still grow greener when you pray

Silver scales flash bright and fade
In reeds along the shore
Like a pearl in sea of liquid jade
His ship comes shining
Like a crystal swan in a sky of suns
His ship comes shining

Mangle the Tango

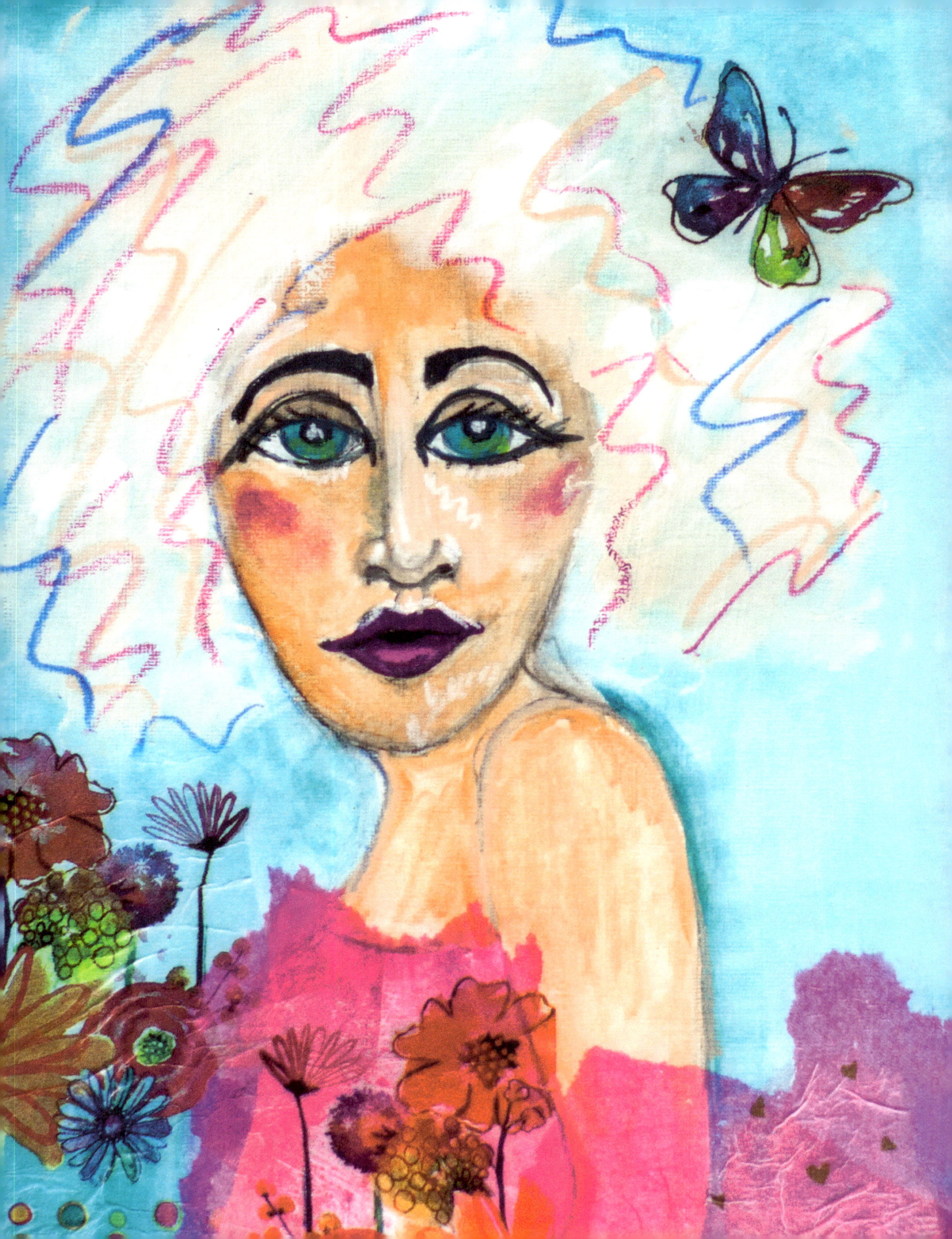

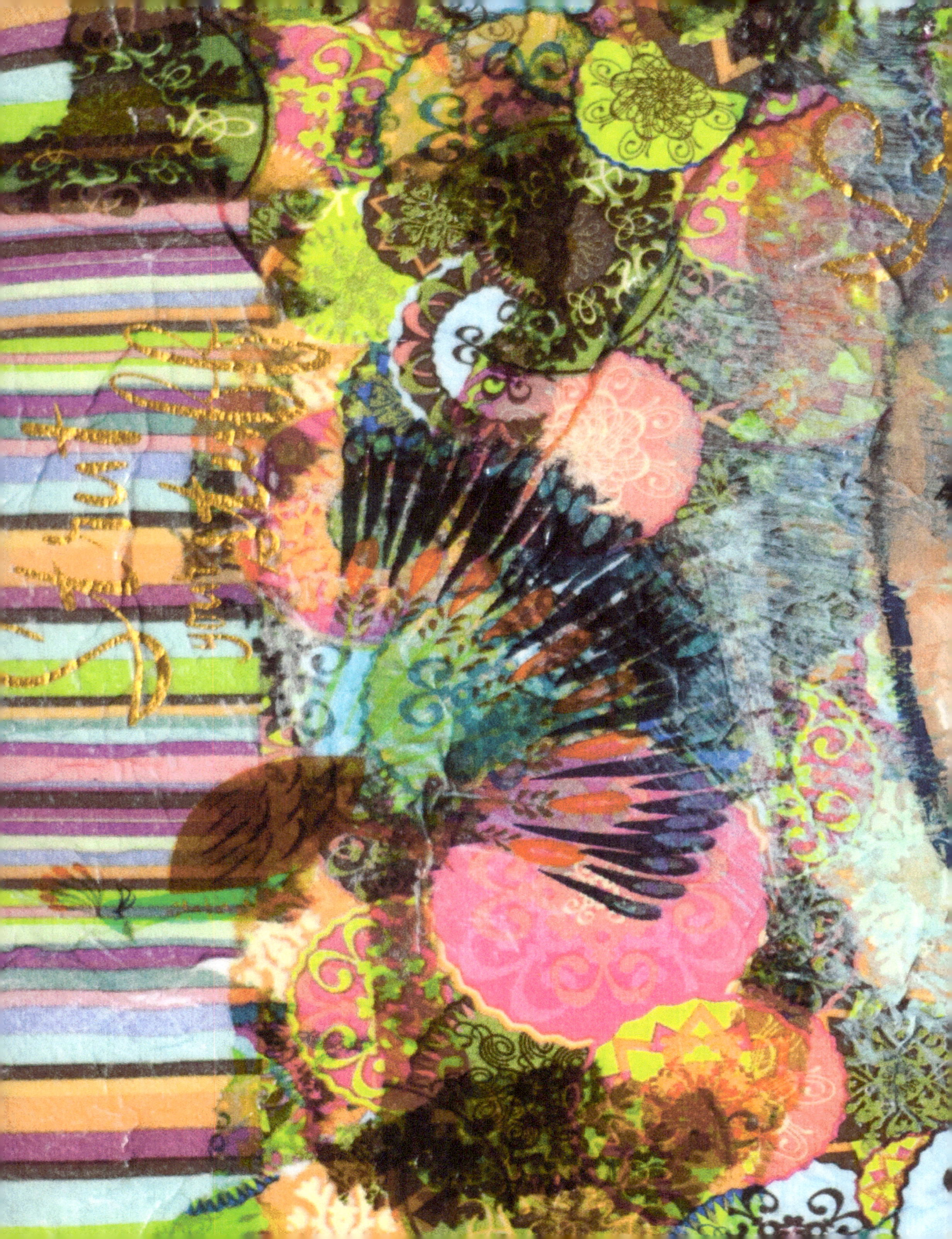

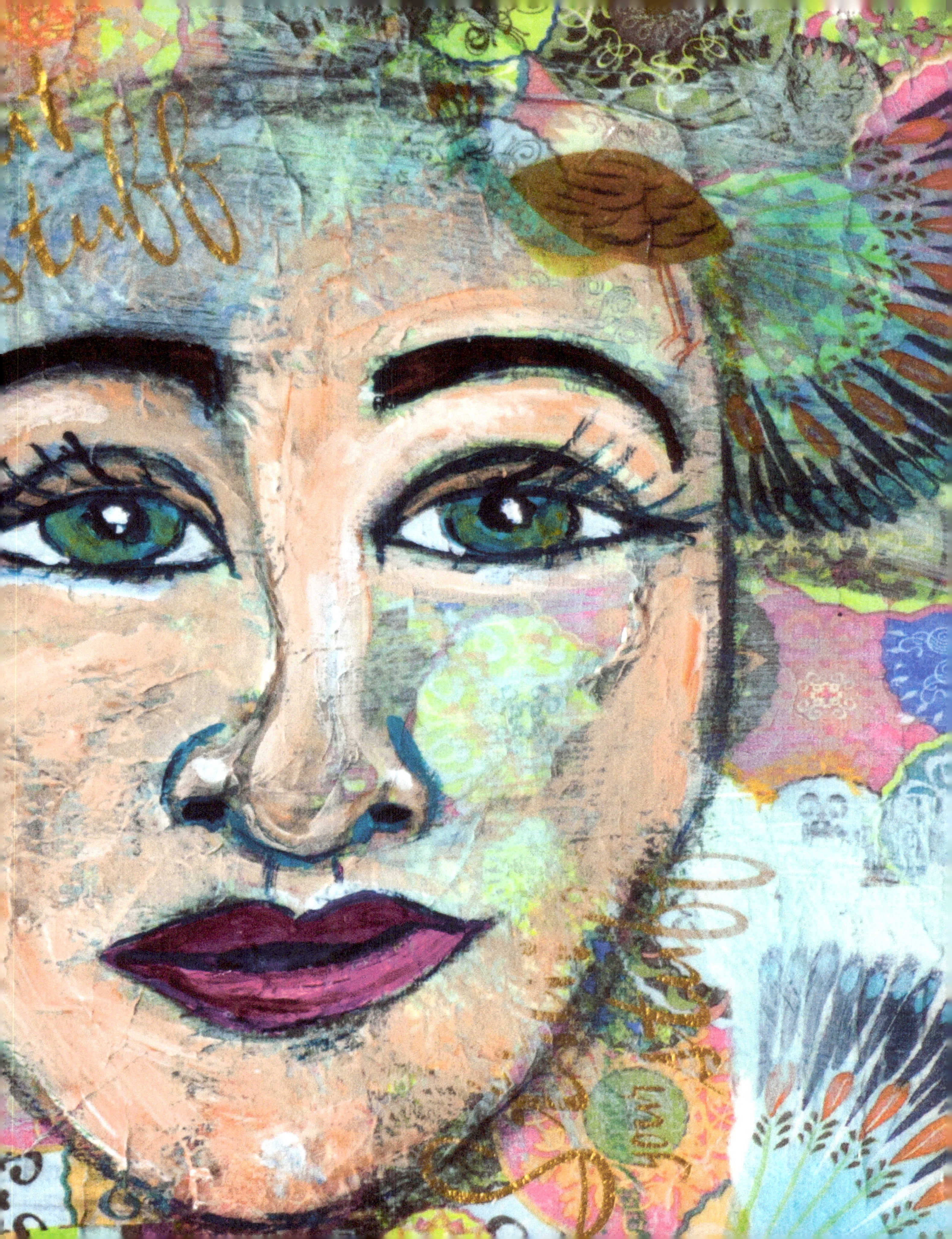
stuff

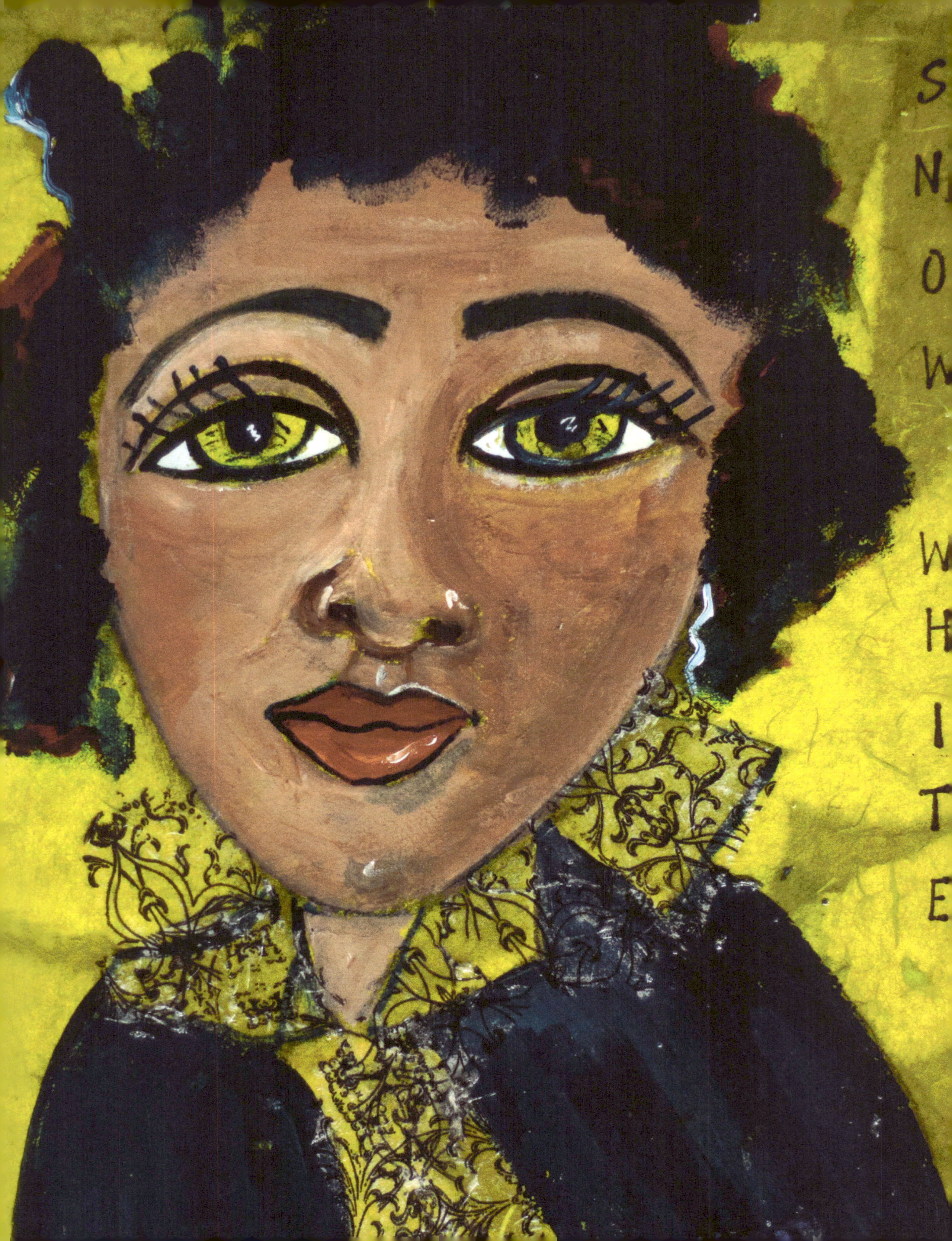

SNOW
WHITE

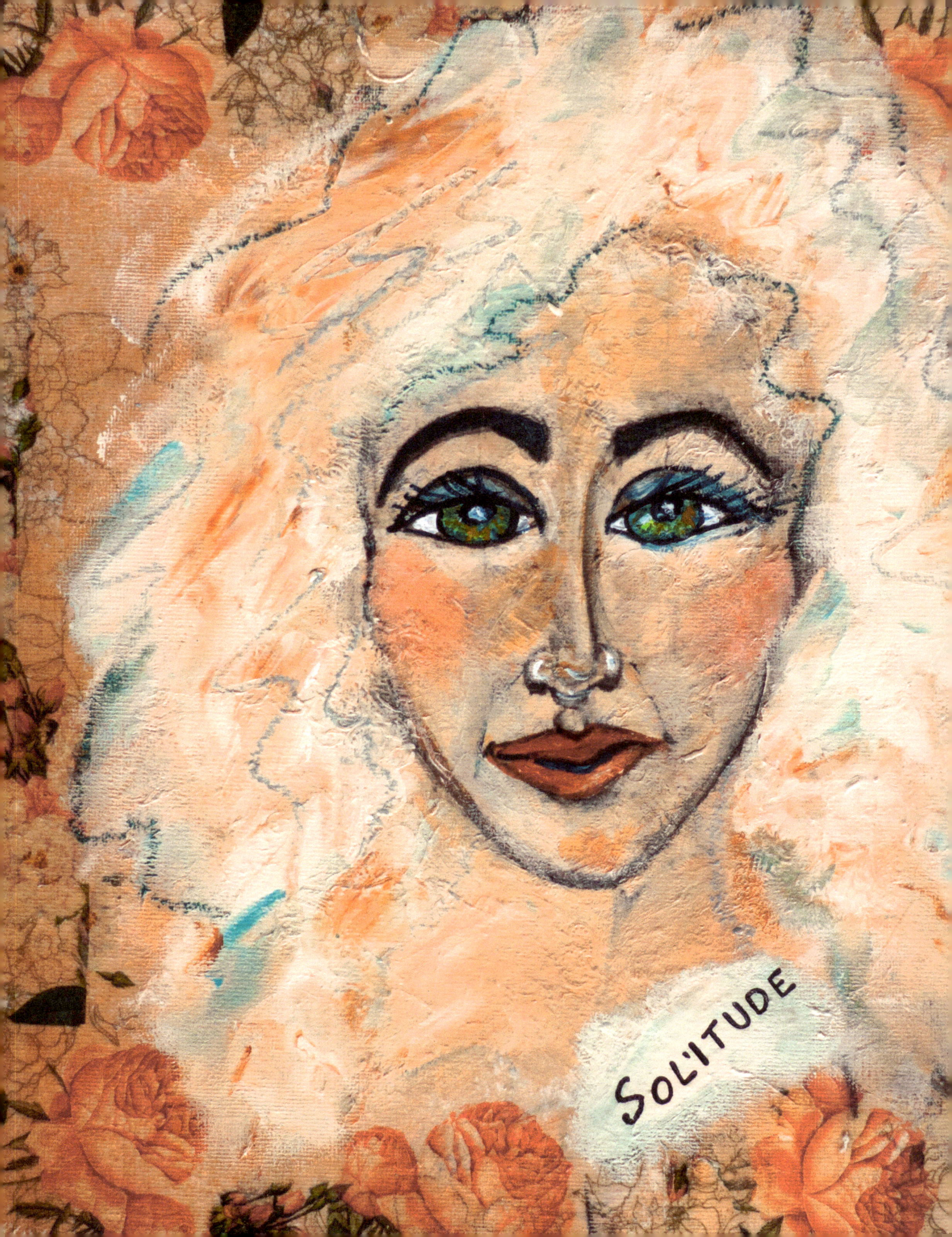
SOLITUDE

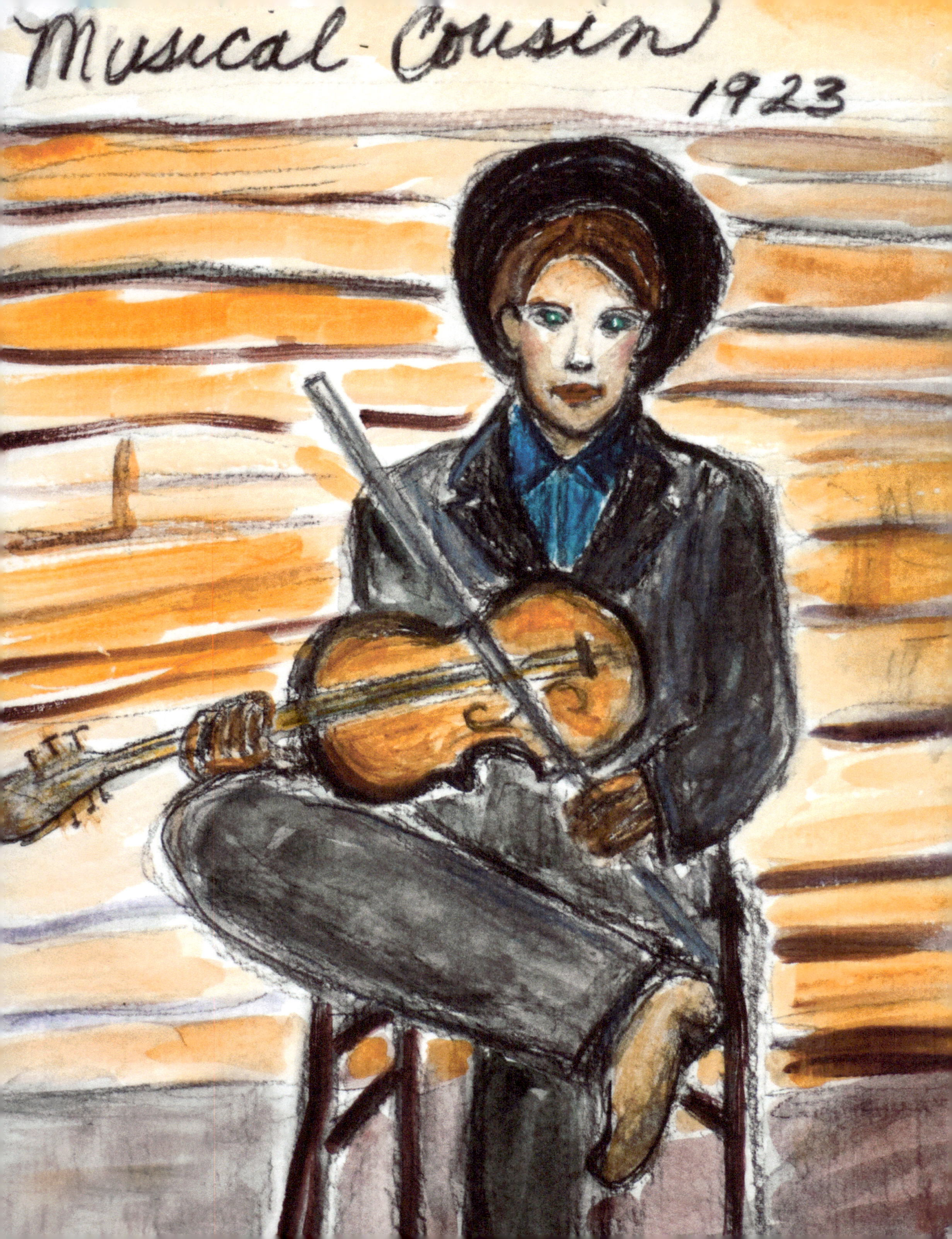

Musical Cousin
1923

ACKNOWLEDGMENTS

I was on the road working as an employee benefits enroller when I had the vision to record "Mangle the Tango."   My friend and mentor, David Bunker, had invited me to a conference hosted by CD Baby in Chicago and our mutual friend Tom Jackson was presenting a seminar on bringing your songs to life on stage.   That same trip David asked me to sing and speak to his students at Visible Music & Arts College about being a professional musician.   The two events reignited by vision of myself as an artist who still has something to offer, even as a boomer entering into those "golden years."

I played David a couple of demos that Roy Salmond, our friend, musician, and producer had produced on me a few years previously and David enthusiastically exclaimed that the songs were fantastic and that Roy really got me. That same night, I called and asked Roy if he'd be interested in producing an album on me in April of 2017 (six months away.) He said yes.

At the same time that I committed to preparing material and my voice for this new album, I also dedicated myself to take a painting class and painting every day as well as writing and rehearsing my material.   I began my regime to prepare for recording the songs for "Mangle the Tango" on January 1.   I took three painting classes in January and then painted as well as rehearsed nearly every day before I went into the studio and while I was in the studio.

I posted all of this information to "PamMarkHall's Tribe" on Facebook and announced a GoFundMe campaign to raise the money for production and manufacturing.   I also began posting my artwork and getting very positive responses to the paintings. Thanks to "PamMarkHall's Tribe" for encouraging me to continue painting and posting as well as to generously funding the campaign to make it possible to bring these two projects to fruition.

I was contacted by my Facebook friend, Creative Director, Tim Gilman, encouraging me to produce a book that would include my song lyrics, the back stories to go along with the songs and some of my paintings.   I loved the idea and Tim graciously offered to handle putting the project together.   He also created a cool logo for my book and record company names: Exhuma Worldwide and Exhuma Records.

This book is a reality because of Tim's vision and commitment to bring it to life.

I am so grateful.

Pam Mark Hall

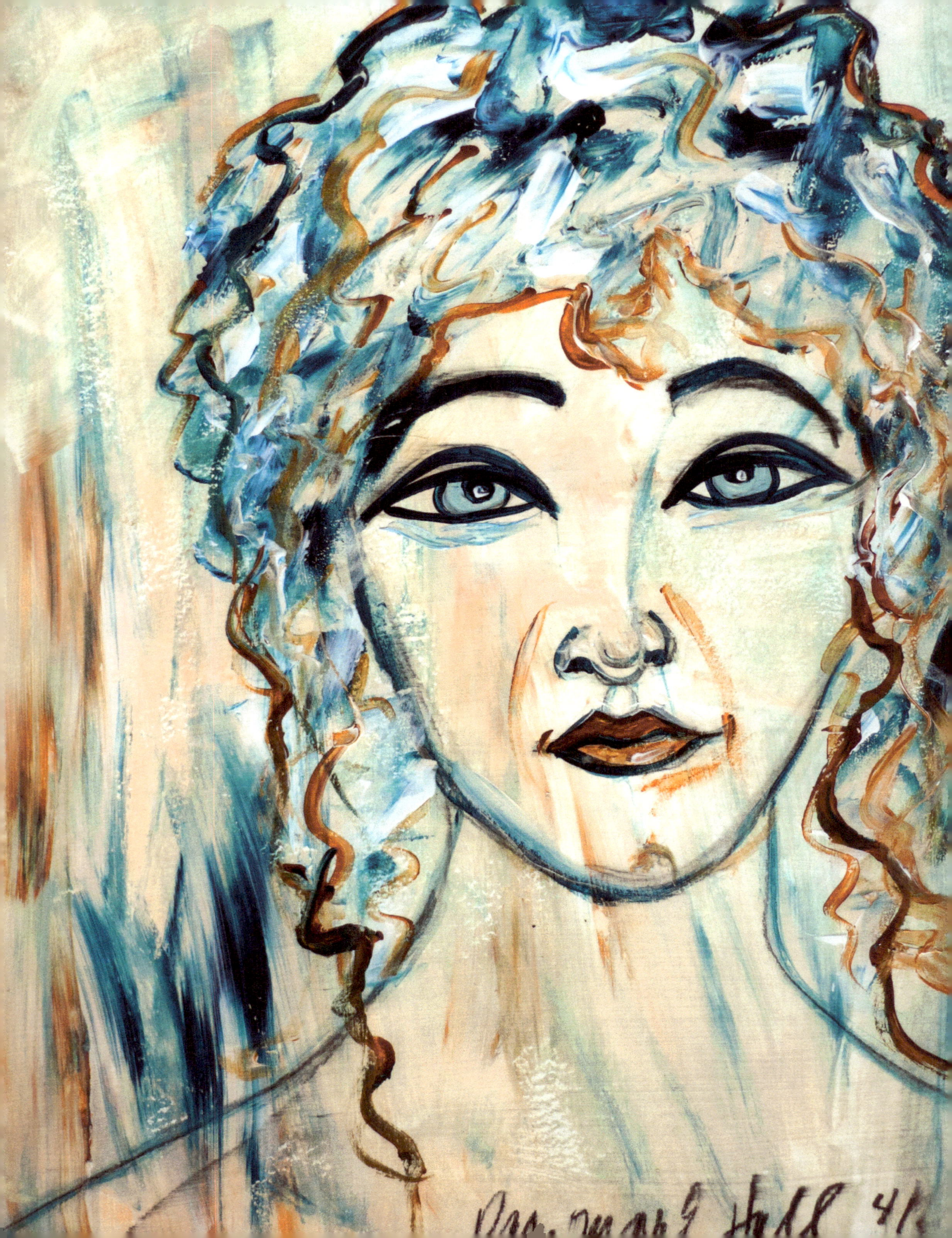

ABOUT THE AUTHOR

Pam Mark Hall is an eclectic critically acclaimed folk/pop/rock singer/songwriter/producer/painter who has been a creative force since her childhood. Blessed with a gift for words that transcend the everyday, her songs are full of startling insights and surprising musical twists and turns. Pam tells stories and sings her songs with convincing passion that cover a wide spectrum of content. This includes the dynamics of human and divine love, pain and struggle, forgiveness, healing and joy. After graduating from Sacramento State University in 1973, Pam worked on staff at Hollywood Presbyterian Church. During 1975 she was an intern at Discovery Arts Guild (an extension of Peninsula Bible Church) in Palo Alto, CA where she also began her recording career. Pam Mark Hall has recorded and commercially released eight albums.

During the 1980s Pam Mark Hall relocated to Nashville when her resonant voice and insightful lyrics were sought after by the burgeoning contemporary Christian music community. Pam is a Grammy and Dove Award nominated artist/producer for her production of the compilation lullaby album Good Night Sleep Tight. A number of her songs have been recorded by well-known musicians including Amy Grant, Debby Boone, Noel Paul Stookey, Sandi Patty and The Imperials. One of her most recognized songs, Sparrow Watcher – a collaboration of Pam with renowned singer/songwriter Rich Mullins, was recorded as a trio with Pam, Amy Grant and Kathy Troccoli. Sparrow Watcher became a top ten hit on CCM radio.

The 1990s was the era Pam worked with the homeless via The Salvation Army, Nashville, as well as abused women and children via the TN Coalition Against Domestic Violence. She became a successful advertising executive in the 2000s and now works as an employee benefits enroller in addition to her concert schedule. Returning to Northern California in 2013 to be near her aging parents, Pam currently performs at house concerts, backyard concerts, churches and assisted living facilities. She paints and creates mixed media pieces. She also gives workshops on creativity and songwriting and says, "Maybe I'm crazy, because while many people my age are eager to retire, I'm inspired to rise from the ashes of life's fiery challenges to share from my resources and experiences." "I'd rather fall than never dance at all. I'd rather Mangle the Tango."

You can reach Pam for bookings at:
pmh@pammarkhall.com

manglethetango.com

www.ingramcontent.com/pod-product-compliance
Lightning Source LLC
Chambersburg PA
CBHW042200030726
47599CB00004B/815